Wilton Place Publishing

Also by Steven E. Browne

The 3by3 Writing Series

Plan, Write and Finish Your Novel - The Workbook

BLOG: https://3by3writingmethod.wordpress.com/

WEBSITE: 3by3writingmethod.com

TWITTER: @3by3writer

FACEBOOK: facebook.com/threebythree.writingmethod

Non-Fiction

The Accident Report

High Definition Post Production

Getting that Job in Hollywood

Video Editing

Introduction to Non-Linear Editing

Film/Video Terms and Concepts

Fiction

Protecting the Source

Holly Would, But Stacy Won't

The 3by3 Writing Method

೪   ೪   ೪   ೪

Plan, Write and Finish Your Novel

೪   ೪   ೪   ೪

The Workbook

Wilton Place Publishing. All rights reserved.
Copyright 2013 Steven E. Browne

Wilton Place Publishing, P.O. Box 291, La Cañada Flintridge, CA 91012

Disclaimer: This is a do-it-yourself guide book. It contains suggestions and ideas about planning and completing a novel. It does not guarantee that following these suggestions someone can or will complete their book. Writing a book is the author's responsibility.

Wilton Place Publishing, the author, and the 3by3 Writing Method do not assume responsibility for other writer's books or their content.

Dedication

To Michele, my wonderful, patient and creative wife without whom this book would not exist.

Table of Contents

* * * * *

* * * * *

Acknowledgments

I want to thank my wonderful children, Nikki, Kris, and Kate who bring joy and happiness to my life.

I'd also like to thank the dedicated and talented members of my Pasadena-based 3by3 Writing Method Meetup group who have listened to me recite these words over and over.

Four brief apologies

One

Many examples within these pages refer to movies. Sometimes it is easier to cite a film seen by millions, than a book few have read.

Two

I have tried to alternate gender assignments to keep the reader on her toes.

Three

The description of the 3by3 Writing Method has been delayed a few chapters so that the reader can get started right away.

If you want to read the overview of the 3by3 Writing Method skip to Chapters Four and Five.

Four

Not everyone wants to know how to publish a book, but many writers need help in finishing their project. The 3by3 Writing Method Workbooks are divided into separate editions. This one is designed to help you complete your manuscript.

Diagram of the 3by3 Writing Method

PLAN, WRITE & FINISH YOUR BOOK

1. Write Daily at a Dedicated Time & Place

2. Constant Contained Conflict (CCC)

3. Finish, a typo-free, properly formatted manuscript

PERSONAL COMMITMENT

7. Clarity

8. Persistence

9. Networking

PUBLISHING YOUR NOVEL

4. Traditional agent/publisher

5. Print-on-demand

6. eBook platforms

Two pages a day equals two drafts a year.

THE 3BY3 WRITING METHOD
PLAN, WRITE AND FINISH YOUR NOVEL

1. Write Daily at a Dedicated Time and Place

> 1.1 Write at the same time every day.

> 1.2 Write in the same place every day.

> 1.3 Work for the same length of time every day.

2. Constant Contained Conflict (CCC)

> 2.1 Characters are conflicted internally.

> 2.2 Characters have conflicts with each other.

> 2.3 Characters have ties to each other; financially, through family or some binding tie that confines and constrains them.

3. Finish a typo-free, properly formatted manuscript

> 3.1 The manuscript is properly formatted and has gone through at least two comprehensive drafts.

> 3.2 The manuscript has been read by at least one reader and/or a critique group familiar with your genre.

> 3.3 At least one professional pass has been made to correct spelling, formatting and grammar.

Chapter One

Million Dollar Bestseller

The 3by3 Writing Method is not a "write a bestseller during your lunch hour" manual. But, if you follow the 3by3 instructions, write every day, in the same place, at the same time, finish several drafts, join one or two critique groups, and have a professional proof-read your book, you can complete your novel and be published.

The goal is to help you:

Write several concise paragraphs that describe the basis of your story, its conflicts and major plot points.

Develop a plot plan with at least fifteen detailed scenes.

Create six balanced characters (three good, three bad) with internal and external conflicts and one conflicted antagonist.

Find reference books and websites that offer help for writing, marketing and publishing your book.

Complete an interesting manuscript, properly formatted and proofread, that you can market or self-publish.

3by3 Writing Method Flow Chart

Of the Writing Process

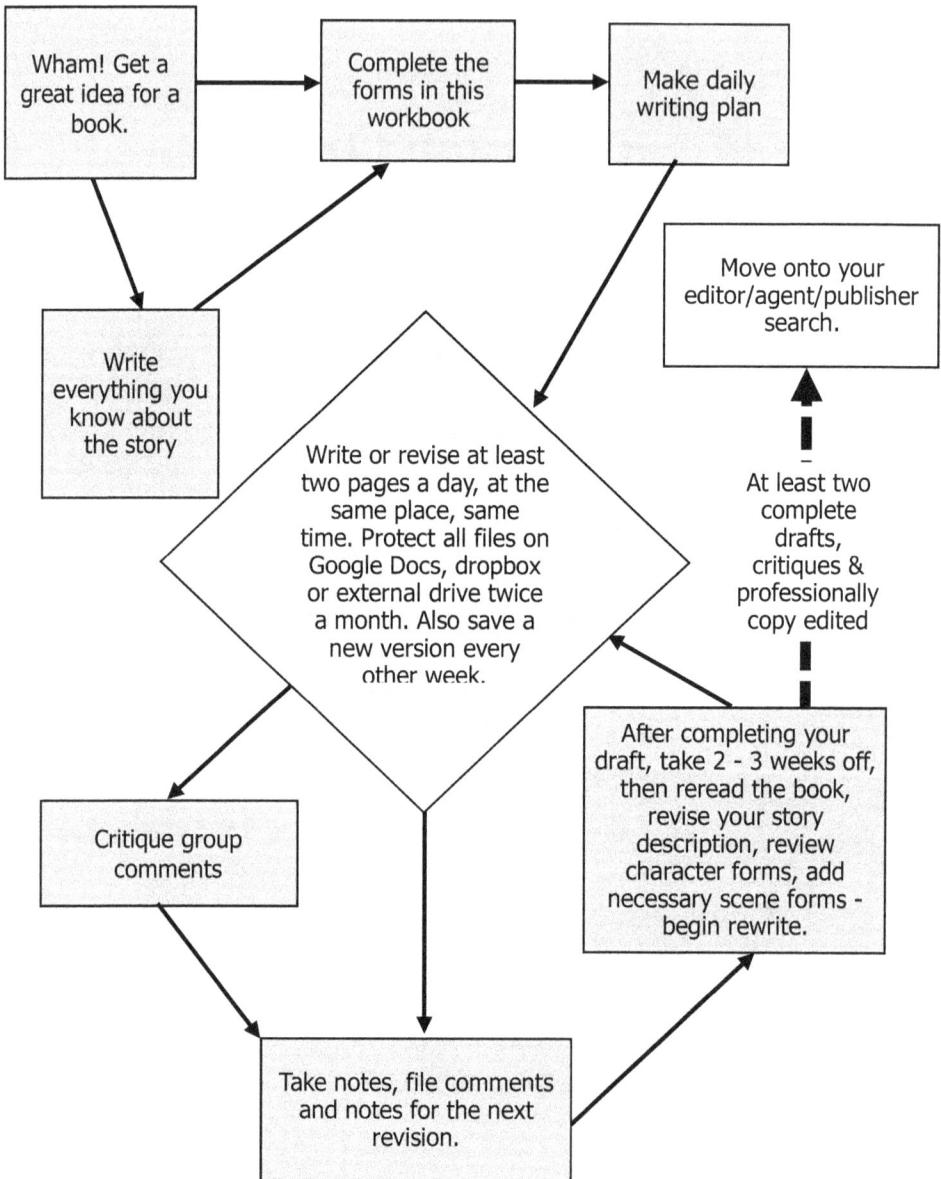

Wham! Get a great idea for a book.

Complete the forms in this workbook

Make daily writing plan

Write everything you know about the story

Move onto your editor/agent/publisher search.

Write or revise at least two pages a day, at the same place, same time. Protect all files on Google Docs, dropbox or external drive twice a month. Also save a new version every other week.

At least two complete drafts, critiques & professionally copy edited

Critique group comments

After completing your draft, take 2 - 3 weeks off, then reread the book, revise your story description, review character forms, add necessary scene forms - begin rewrite.

Take notes, file comments and notes for the next revision.

Chapter Two

The Marathon

I was working on my third novel, my twelfth book, churning out lots of paragraphs and chapters. I thought I had it all under control. Then it happened. I crashed into the dreaded writer's block. Stalled at 150 pages I was unhappy with what I'd written and had no idea know how my story ended.

It took a variety of events and several years of exploring my internal motives to bring the 3by3 Writing Method into focus.

As a result of that journey, I created a guide to help a committed writer produce a finished, interesting book that could be published.

I also came to the conclusion that:

You cannot write a novel by just sitting down and writing.

The Writing Marathon

Deciding to write a book is like deciding to run a marathon. Preparation is required. There must be commitment. You need to know the route you are traveling and you have to the location of the finish line **before** you start.

Many beginning novelists believe you must sit for hours making up everything as you go. Certainly a novel requires a great deal of time, but it's not realistic to think you can plant yourself in front of a keyboard and simply "write a book."

There are probably a few individuals who can whip out a 300 page manuscript without any planning, but those people are extremely gifted. If you're reading this manual, you probably aren't one of them.

For the average person a "damn it, I'll just write" simply does not work.

Hikers plan. Builders plan. Sailors plan. Airline pilots plan. Runners know the route - all the way to the end.

Chapter Three

Let's Go!

You're in a hurry. You have a great idea. You bought this guide to help write your novel. Without further delay, here we go.

How To Use This Workbook

Obviously, you can use this text any way you chose. My suggestion would be to be to read it straight through and complete each fill-in-the-blank form that you encounter along the way.

After reading the book front to back, I would then recommend making copies of all the work you've done and put those pages into a three ring binder.

Skipping the written information contained in this manual will most likely get you where you are now...and you know why you bought this workbook.

General Story Plan

If you don't take the time to create a story plan, your writing will probably grind to a halt. That heady emotion you once felt will most likely fade. Then there's a good chance your partially finished book will become like so many others, thrown in a drawer with sadness and regret.

It doesn't have to be that way. If you know where your story is headed and how it ends, your manuscript can be finished in a reasonable amount of time.

In order to create a general plot, you will need to fill in the blanks along the way. When you've finished this workbook you will know exactly what to write.

"I don't need to do that. I have a great story," you say.

Good. Then filling in the form will be easy.

Then you say, "I don't need to do this. My idea is awesome."

An idea is not a story unless it has a beginning, a middle and an end. You also need to define your character's goal and conflicts. Fill in the form and your story will take shape.

And if you're thinking something like "It's a story's about a guy who invents the next Velcro and then someone steals it." That's not a story and you definitely need to fill out the form.

If you're concerned that you'll forget all the details about your idea while answering these questions, get a pad or open a file in on your computer and write everything you know about your story, then return to filling out all the forms in this workbook.

Pencils at Work

I strongly suggest using a pencil as you progress through the exercises. During the process of writing one book, a new one often emerges. A pencil and eraser make changes much cheaper and easier than buying another workbook.

MAIN CHARACTER/PLOT FORM

Answering the following questions will help you define your story. You can go back and rework your answers until your idea sounds plausible, but resist the temptation to dive in and start writing. You'll have more than enough work...once you know what to do.

Main character's age and gender

A character's age determines how he will act and react. A fifteen-year-old male is a much different person than a forty year old female. An elderly widow has needs and interests unlike those of a twenty-five-year-old coed.

My main character is a _____ (**age**) year-old _____. (Man, woman, girl, boy, dog, dragon, butterfly)

Main Character's Occupation

Even if your main character's profession is never used or mentioned, what he does (or did) is extremely important to your story. You must know your character's background, experience and skills.

The main character in my story is/was a _____. (**occupation** – architect, priest, teacher, graphic arts student, comedian, construction worker, career criminal, weightlifter, hotel clerk, homeless woman, Wall Street trader, salesman, meter maid, CEO, alcoholic housewife, pilot.)

Main Character's Beginning Emotional Status

Your main character has an intense emotional state that is extremely important to your story. This emotion will change over the course of the book and is usually one of the first aspects to be revealed.

At the beginning of the story my main character is

_____   _____. (**beginning**

emotional status – unhappy, crazy, lonely, in love, desperate,

greedy, mean, happy, cocky, stupid, naïve, extremely vain,

gifted, innocent, possessed, strung out, dead, challenged,

frustrated with his illness, angry about his situation)

The Trigger Event

Early in your story (not necessarily at the start of your book) something happens to your main character. This is called the "**trigger event**." Sometimes this trigger event has an immediate impact on the main character. Other times it affects him later in the story. This trigger event can happen "off-screen" and create a situation later in his life.

Sometimes the trigger event does not happen to the main character. It could be that a beloved cheerleader is kidnapped, a girl in high school humiliates him, or an asteroid is going to destroy the earth. It could be that a pet mouse is suddenly able to predict the stock market.

There are times when we don't learn about the trigger event until the end of the story, but most often it occurs at or near the beginning. The trigger event is always some kind of action.

What happens to my main character is that

_____ _____.

(**trigger event** – he gets beat-up, his spouse goes into a coma, is stood up on prom night, buys a gun, she witnesses a crime, a volcano erupts in his backyard, he finds a thousand dollars, he's hit by a car, his parents are killed by storm troopers, she sees a body fall from a roof, a tsunami hits her hotel, he is abducted by very small aliens, he volunteers for the Army, she meets an incredibly attractive person, he is offered a weird job).

Main Character's Goal

Early in your story, your character will **decide that he wants something**. This decision usually comes after the trigger event and this **goal** will be present throughout your book.

In some stories this goal is monumental, like saving humanity from the oncoming asteroid. In other stories it can be fraught with danger, like rescuing a child from a ruthless kidnapper. Perhaps it is simply to be kissed by the boy of her dreams at the prom.

No matter how big or small your story, your main character must have a goal - a goal that is incredibly important to that character.

It is significant to note that the main character's original goal may never be realized. However, that original burning desire is the motivation that sends her on a journey - which is the story of your book.

My main character decides _____

_____ (**main character's goal** –
to fall in love, be an NFL quarterback, reconcile with his ex-
wife, make millions of dollars, kill the evil emperor, avenge the
death of his wife and child, save the world in order that his
daughter has a life, save the princess so he can marry her,
become the class president, be the best juggler in southern
Kansas.)

Main Character's First Major Action

The trigger event will cause your main character to choose a
goal and then act. In some stories this **first major action** is
extreme and out of character, like a fireman starting a fire in his
own home. In other situations this reaction is within the
character's normal activities, like a fireman responding to a fire
with his fellow firefighters.

The action that results from the trigger event has to make sense.
If a person has failed a final exam in junior high school, she
usually doesn't run off and rob banks in Argentina.

The **first major action** does not have to be earthshaking or
monumental. A person's life is filled with interesting and
touching moments, from the marriage of a good friend, to
meeting an influential person, to getting rejected by your first-
choice college. A trigger event can be small and "insignificant"
from a world view, but it is always very, very important to your
main character.

The answer to this statement is the main character's first action, a verb.

As a result of _____

(**trigger event**) my main character decides _____

_____ (**main character's goal**) and as a result

_____ (**first major action** – exercises a

lot, agrees to fly to the asteroid and destroy it, goes on a blind

date, shoots a friend, buys a race car, raises an evil spirit, rises

from the dead, hides from the mob, brags about winning the

lottery, asks him out on a date, tries to stop his brother from

murdering a neighbor).

There will be many twists and turns, triumphs and failures as your main character tries to reach his goal and the antagonist's people try to stop him. That is the body of your book. In this chapter we're only dealing with the major aspects of your story.

Main Character's Changed or Intensified Emotional State

In order for your progress to develop, your main character's emotions must change or intensify. This changed or intensified emotional state usually causes your main character to alter her approach to her original goal and eventually results in a final action.

Here are some examples of the changed or intensified emotions that occur in popular movies.

In "Avatar" Jake Sully realizes the military is wrong and changes his allegiance to the Na'vi tribe.

In "The Wizard of Oz" Dorothy changes her mind and decides she wants to go home.

In "Iron Man" Tony Stark realizes his partner has double-crossed him and is endangering the world so he risks his life to stop him.

In Tim Burton's "Alice in Wonderland" Alice decides to help her friends and fight the Jabberwocky.

My main character's new or intensified emotional state is when he/she makes a new decision to _____

_____. (**Changed or intensified emotional state –** be extremely jealous, change his loyalty, go after his first love, commit to sobriety, find the real criminal, defeat the evil aliens, go to the prom with his neighbor, realize he does love her, decide the city was wrong and help the homeowner.)

The Final Action

The main character's changed emotional state will cause him to do many things and go many places. Toward the end of the story he will perform a final action.

Often the final action is also the final confrontation with the individual who has been blocking his attempt at reaching his goal.

As a result of my character's new or greatly intensified emotional state, he/she _____
(**final action** – gets married, climbs that mountain, apologizes to her, buys a diamond ring, goes on vacation, gives up smoking, sacrifices his life for his daughter, blows up the plane, accepts the job, goes to a different college, kills the bad guy)

The Final Consequence

The main character's final action produces a final consequence. This major action (either emotional or physical) occurs at the climax of the story.

The main character's actions toward achieving his/her goal causes _____ _____ _____ (**final consequence** – the world to be doomed, all the agents in the Matrix to be destroyed, the Empire's Death Star to blow up, the girl of his dreams to kiss him, him to get his diary back, him to be accepted into the honors program at Yale, her to win the scholarship.)

The Revelation

After the final action and resulting consequence, there is a **revelation**. Many times it is the main character who makes this observation. In some cases, the main character has moved on, or is dead. In this case, the survivors come to the final conclusion.

This revelation, or discovery, is the culmination of the main character's evolution as she heads toward her goal and confronts many challenges. In most cases, this revelation is also the underlying theme that runs throughout the story.

13

As a result of the main character's actions she discovers

_____ _____.

(**revelation** – settling down is the right thing to do, the force is real, being right is not always profitable, parenthood is difficult but worth it, love requires painful sacrifice, they really were heroes, the killers are his only friends, death is part of life, you don't always get what you want, politicians are liars, no risk - no reward, you really can win at poker, love conquers all.)

Main Character's Name

Now that you have an idea of what's going to happen in your story and to your main character, it is time to choose a name. When choosing the main character's name, you might want to foreshadow the story's plot or give an indication of the main character's challenge.

Ricky Love (romance)   Luke Skywalker (space pilot)

Jason Banks (finance)   Lance Daze (fencing expert)

Jessie Beach (swimmer)   Kelly Trublood (vampire)

There should be something special about your main character's name. So after giving it some thought:

My main character's full name is _____

_____.

The Antagonist

There's always a bad guy (or girl) in any successful story. It doesn't matter if she's the nasty cheerleader, the Terminator, a dishonest teacher, the stalker, or the evil corporate leader. The antagonist attempts to block the main character from his goal.

Sometimes the antagonist is the agent of the Matrix. Sometimes it is the bully of the school. Other times the antagonist is the rival family leader vying for power (and who plays dirty).

The main character always fights SOMEONE - a person. The main character cannot fight the entire the police department. He has to fight the police chief or the mayor. The members of the police can alter their position if the boss changes his mind or is eliminated.

Without the foil, the main character would accomplish her goal in a few pages. It doesn't work that way in a story. The main character has to struggle against Darth Vader, the mean girls, the Jabberwocky, or the Wicked Witch of the West.

In "Fight Club," when the character is actually fighting himself, the story portrays that alter-ego as a separate character.

In "The Help" everyone is in conflict with everyone, but only one character personifies the racist attitude of the town.

The antagonist must have a reason to stop the main character. It could be that the evil witch wants to be "fairest of them all" or that if the main character succeeds, the antagonist will be fingered as the real murderer.

In many stories the antagonist is an authority figure with outdated or unjust opinions. Perhaps she wants to be in control and the main character is threatening that position.

On the other hand, the main character usually doesn't care about these morals, the antagonist's evil deeds or unwritten social rules. She just wants to achieve her goal which is vital to her character.

Your antagonist may not show up until later in the story, but the ultimate showdown will eventually occur between the antagonist and the main character to provide a climatic confrontation.

The Antagonist in my story is _____

and hates and/or blocks my main character because

_____.

THE STORY DESCRIPTION IN A PARAGRAPH

The next step is to create a description of your story using the information from the previous questions. This description will define your story plot and main character's actions. Using the answers from the earlier pages, complete the following sentence.

_____ (**name**) a _____

(**age**) year old _____ (**occupation**) was feeling

_____ (**beginning emotion**).

Then _____ (**trigger action**)

and as a result he makes up his mind to

_____ (**goal**) and as a result

_____. (**first action**)

The character who most wants to stop _____

(**main character**) is _____

(**the antagonist**) because _____

_____ _____. (**reason for hating**

or blocking the main character)

_____ (**main character**) becomes

_____ (**intense emotional state**) and he

_____ (**final action**) which results in

_____ (**final result**) and discovers

_____. (**revelation**)

YOUR STORY

Next create a story summary using your own words. Read it out loud. Does it make sense? Does your character learn anything? Is it interesting? Make sure this is the story you want to write for the next year of your life. If it isn't right, work on it some more.

You <u>Have</u> to Know the Ending

Do not even think that you can figure out your ending after you start writing. You **must** take the time to plan your entire story right now. Not knowing your ending before you start is a sure-fire way to fail. If you use the 3by3 Writing Method, **you have to know how your book ends before you begin writing** or you risk not finishing.

Your ending may change during the process, and most likely will be altered somewhat in the second draft but you have to know your ending now, before you begin.

The following story description is an example of a book concept.

Run Rick Run - Plot Synopsis

Thirty-six-year-old ex-marine Rick Powers is broke, dealing with memories of his ex-girlfriend and has lost his beloved dog, Mojo. When a wealthy college friend invites him to a black-tie party and hints at lucrative job offer, Rick accepts.

In the hotel bar, Rick meets gorgeous, but clumsy Stacy Gunnison. They immediately hit it off and sneak off to her suite. Later, Rick is offered thousands to deliver a small package to the nearby airport.

Suspicious of the toothless messenger, Rick tries to back out of the deal, but a hard-of-hearing Asian assassin, "Blade deSlasher" mistakes Rick Powers for the famous agent, Rick Flowers. More spies join in the chase for the valuable device that Rick hides in numerous places including a Taco Bell take-out container and Stacy's water bra.

Throughout the night Stacy and Rick are shot at, tied up, involved in a deadly golf cart race, and witness to a dozen incredibly bizarre murders. Rick realizes he thoroughly enjoys Stacy, despite her questionable background and remarkable high-tech weapons. He ends up rescuing her from a variety of badly dressed villains and finds his missing Mojo.

Finally, Rick puts himself in a no-win situation in order to save Stacy and protect top-secret military data. In an explosive finale, he discovers he's more powerful than he thought possible, that love is blind, and it really, really hurts to get shot.

This story might not sell to a big New York publisher, but it has a beginning, a middle and an end. Before the final draft is completed this story will definitely be reworked, but there's character growth and a change in attitude. Rick moves from acting like a loser to a man on a mission with hope and self-confidence.

Your Main Character has a Problem

A main character must have at least two significant issues. One is trying to achieve her goal. The second is an internal, personal conflict.

This personal problem could be a fear of germs, insecurities with dating strangers, singing in public, fear of stepping on sidewalk cracks, the color red, or, heaven forbid, a fear of books. Other characters often use the main character's internal issue to their advantage. This internal problem makes the main character vulnerable and more interesting to the reader.

During your story, the main character is constantly challenged by these two issues, one internal and one external.

My character's internal problem is:

_____ _____.

Now you have the basis of a story.

Before we develop your supporting characters and the many conflicts within your story, we are going to spend a little time to explain the 3by3 Writing Method.

Chapter Four

What is the 3by3 Writing Method?

The 3by3 Writing Method is a process designed to help an author plan, write, finish and then publish an interesting, professional-quality book. The process has 3 major sections. Each section has 3 parts, hence the name 3by3.

Section One – Writing the Book

This first section is about planning writing and completing a book of sufficient quality (several drafts with no typos or grammatical errors) to submit to agents and publishers. Here are the three parts of section one.

1. A dedicated time and space for writing

      1.1 Write at the same time every day.

      1.2 Write in the same place every day.

      1.3 Work for the same length of time every day.

2. Constant Contained Conflict (CCC)

   2.1 Characters are conflicted internally.

   2.2 Characters have conflicts with each other.

   2.3 Characters have ties to each other; financially, through family or some binding tie that confines and constrains them.

3. Finish a typo-free, properly formatted manuscript

   3.1 The manuscript is properly formatted and has gone through at least two comprehensive drafts.

   3.2 The manuscript has been read by at least one reader and/or a critique group familiar with your genre.

   3.3 At least one professional pass has been made to correct spelling, formatting and grammar.

Section Two — Publishing

This second portion of the 3by3 Writing Method describes the three major publishing avenues and how to get your book into the hands of readers.

The 3by3 Writing Method always supports and aims at traditional publishing as a first option. An experienced, reputable publisher can offer far more sales and marketing opportunities than an individual trying to "go it alone" with self-publishing.

Unfortunately, only a very small percentage of writers will be accepted for publication using the traditional agent/publisher route.

Once appropriate publishers and agents have been approached and queries have been sent, the finished manuscript as well as support materials are prepared for print-on-demand (POD) and eBook publication.

If an acceptance for representation or publication is acquired, a portion of the self-publishing process is put on hold, but the preparation of support materials and use of social networking continues. These materials and contacts will be needed no matter who publishes your book.

It is important to understand that agent representation does not guarantee income or publication. You may have to return to the self-publishing option.

4. Traditional Publishers

    4.1 Agent search — heading toward a publisher.

    4.2 Non-agented publisher search.

    4.3 Final attempt at traditional Publishing.

5. Print-on-demand (POD) options.

    5.1 Full-service POD companies.

    5.2 Do-it-yourself options.

    5.3 Middle-of-the-road plans.

6. eBook publishing platforms

    6.1 eBook versus print.

    6.2 Separate platforms.

    6.3 Smashwords.

Section Three – Personal Commitment

Writing a dynamic, enticing manuscript is not enough to sell a book in today's highly competitive environment, no matter who publishes it

The Personal Commitment section of the 3by3 Writing Method is designed to help the author get his books noticed allowing it the most media awareness possible.

7. Clarity

    7.1 Knowing your market and your audience.

    7.2 Staying focused on your goal.

    7.3 Making a plan and sticking to it.

8. Persistence

    8.1 Ignoring the temptation to quit.

    8.2 Always be watching, reading and aware.

    8.3 Working through the doldrums, discouragement, frustrations and loneliness.

9. Networking

    9.1 Continually make friends with industry people and your future audience.

    9.2 Give as much as you take (karma works).

    9.3 Conferences, critiques, meetings.

Great ideas need a plan

Inspiration for a great book can come from many places. It could be an amazing life experience, an overheard story, a nightmare, a bizarre image you imagine as you fall asleep, or a late night of brainstorming that produces scribbles on a stained napkin.

But if a writer begins his book-writing journey without a plan that includes a beginning, a middle and an end, the dreaded "What happens next?" will eventually sneak up and send him walking around the block trying to figure a way out of his dead-end story.

The 3by3 Writing Method can aid in creating an interesting plot with enough conflict and direction that it will motivate a writer to finish her book.

The Personal Ingredient

New friends, professional bonds, and a sense of accomplishment are just a few of the rewards an author can experience.

There is an incredibly special moment when a writer's book is available to the public to read. The 3by3 Writing Method hopes that you experience that feeling.

New Rules

Listed below are a few of the author's favorite and is passing them along.

General Rules

Do not duplicate first letters of character name (no Steve, Sean, Susan and Sally, except for humor or plot purpose).

Write daily even if you don't "feel it."

Your own internal conflicts and feelings can be a source of a positive writing session.

Know your story ending before you start.

Set a realistic deadline and stick to it.

Write or revise at least two pages a day, every day.

Join a critique group to see how you're doing and socialize with other writers.

You can definitely be published.

Browne's Dos

Do go to a writer's conference (even if you haven't finished).

Do use a word processor like MS Word of Open Office text document.

Do put a limit on your writing time (20 minutes to 2 hours before breaking).

Do make a rough plan for the next day's work before you stop.

Do protect your entire manuscript folder every two weeks (Google Docs, Dropbox, external drive or flash drive).

Do tell people that you are writing a book and then try to explain it in three or four paragraphs. (watch for the part when they get bored)

Do read other books of your genre or style.

Do join a critique group and/or writer's social group.

Do take a substantial (2 - 4 weeks) break after finishing a draft before starting a rewrite (distance keeps the vision clear).

Do put your writing schedule on a calendar.

Browne's Don'ts

Don't give or email your entire book to anyone during your creative writing process.

Don't take a break until you completely finish an entire draft.

Don't take criticism personally.

Don't argue or defend criticism, just listen.

Don't give your book to any family members or friends until it is ready to send it to an agent.

Don't constantly rewrite the first few chapters.

Don't get drunk and write. You could hurt someone you love.

Don't constantly spellcheck or count words, just write.

Chapter Five

Writing Time

Write Every Day — Same Place, Same Time

The first requirement of the 3by3 Writing Method is a firm commitment to writing at a specific time and location every day. There is no easy way around this challenge. Although the 3by3 Writing Method can help an aspiring or experienced author to plan, write and complete their novel, the work of creating and checking at least two pages a day falls solely on the writer.

Where does one find the time to write a book? For some it's in the early morning before everyone else's day begins. For others it's in the back of a minivan after dropping the kids off at soccer practice. For still others, it is at the end of a daily lunch. Some writers find time after the kids leave for school. Some stay up late.

This dedicated writing time and place should remain the same. There should be no new sounds, no new keyboards, no checking emails during writing time. The mind needs to be in the same basic thought pattern at each session so there is no ramp-up time.

This concept is so important that the first part of the entire 3by3 Writing Method is about the commitment to writing at the same time and place.

The time may not be long. It could be as short as twenty minutes.

But, this is...

<u>THE</u> WRITING TIME

The writing time can take place at a desk, a chair, or on a park bench. It can be at home, a library, or in the garage. A book contains thousands of words, hundreds of pages. You need a place to create all this.

Producing two pages a day will result in creating or revising over 700 pages a year, in excess of 175,000 words. This is more than enough material for two complete drafts of a 300 page manuscript.

No other computer program can be open. There can be no email, no Facebook, no IMs, no solitaire, no Skype. There can be no tweeting or phone calls.

Every day a minimum of 500 words or two double-spaced pages must be created or revised until the first draft is complete. Some writers have more time or energy, and 1000 or 1500 words can be accomplished in a daily session. The driving force here is to follow your plot path, write your scenes, and do not go back to revise anything except the previous day's work.

Write every day at the same time...

In the same place...

For the same length of time.

It is a good idea to keep a pen and pad handy while writing. Make notes about ideas for settings and character traits, as well as future plot complications that come to mind during your writing session. If you do not write these ideas on paper they often fade as you return your writing tasks.

A Writing Habit

Humans love routines. We set driving routes. We follow holiday and hygiene routines. One of the reasons some people accomplish so many things is that they follow a daily ritual, making daily forward progress, no matter how small. This is also true of the committed writer. A daily routine eliminates time for settling into place, fussing with equipment or "finding the time" to write.

Binge writing - trying to mass-produce pages during random opportunities, usually does not work. Sure, a lot of pages can be whipped out in a few Saturday sessions, but miss one or two, then guilt and despair can set in. This usually is followed by blame, shame and loss of story detail. To avoid this situation, follow the simple formula of short writing periods, every day at the same place.

My writing time will be at _____.

(time of day)

I am going to write for _____. **(minutes daily)**

I will write at _____.

(location).

Post this commitment somewhere where you can see it every day.

There are days you just don't want to

Some days you don't want to get up or you don't want to write that love scene because you're angry at your spouse. Perhaps you don't want to face another day on Chapter Five because Chapter Six is much more interesting. You don't want to write today because you had WAY too much fun the night before.

But you have to. Every day. That's who you are. That's what you like, and that's the only way you're going to get finished. Why? Because you are a writer.

Writing every day at the same place at the same time will become a habit that will be hard to break.

How to write a novel in 12 days.

There is a secret to writing a book in less than two weeks. It is simple and direct. There are no gimmicks involved.

The secret to writing a book in 12 days is revealed on the following page.

The secret to writing a book in 12 days is:

YOU CAN'T.

YOU CANNOT WRITE A QUALITY NOVEL IN TWO WEEKS!

Even if you wrote brilliantly at the rate of two pages an hour, ten hours a day (which is a pretty good clip) that's twenty pages a day, 140 pages a week.

It would take at least sixteen days to complete a first draft. At that point you would still have to read it, revise it, spell-check and have it copy-edited. So, even a phenomenally gifted writer would still need almost month to complete her book.

I'm guessing you're not quite that good, so you'd better budget two pages a day. That way you can write two full drafts in a year.

No matter how fast you go, all that work will take much longer than 12 days!

The Writing Schedule

At this point it would be a good idea to create a calendar or a spread-sheet specifically designed for your book. You could post your schedule on your refrigerator or somewhere in your writing space. You should refer to this plan at least once a week. Below is a sample schedule you might consider using.

Week 1

Pick your writing place, complete the main character/plot form, character name, work on and finish the fill-in-the-blank paragraph then write your own.

Week 2

Complete the seven character forms, 15+ scene forms.

Weeks 3-10

Write two pages a day on your manuscript = approximately 112 pages.

Weeks 11-22

Two pages a day = 165 + 96 = approximately 277 pages; join one social writer's group, search for a critique group

Weeks 22-26

Two pages a day = 70 + 277 = 347 pages, try a critique group.

Week 27-28

Take a break for several weeks. Around the beginning of week 29 reread book from start to finish, making notes from rewrites and critique groups.

On the following page is a similar schedule that allows you to "catch up" to the "two pages a day word" count. These catch-ups are not a week off, just days to allow you to keep on track.

DATE	WEEK	JOB	✓	DATE	WEEK	JOB	✓
	1	Pick the writing place, do main character description, plot form, story description			14	Pages 141- 154	
	2	Complete seven character cards, 15+ scene cards.			15	Pages 155 - 168	
	3	Pages 1 - 14			16	Pages 169 - 182	
	4	Pages 15 - 28			17	Pages 183 - 196	
	5	Pages 29 - 42			18	Catch up, visit a critique group	
	6	Pages 43 - 56			19	Pages 197 - 210	
	7	Pages 57 - 70			20	Pages 211 - 224	
	8	Pages 71 - 84			21	Pages 225 - 238	
	8	Pages 85 - 98			22	Pages 239 - 252	
	10	Pages 99 - 112			23	Pages 253- 266	
	11	Catch up, search for a critique group			24	Pages 267- 280	
	12	Pages 113 - 126			25	Pages 281 - 294	
	13	Pages 127 - 140			26	Pages 295 - 308	

Commitment vs. Punishment

You missed a day. You feel like you're falling behind. This is no reason to toss everything or worry that you'll never finish. Remorse does not help when writing a book. Simply return to your writing routine as soon as possible.

In the Writing Place - First Draft

Let's go over a twenty minute writing session to give you an idea of what might take in order a day's work.

7:00 - 7:04 - - review notes for today plot today's pages.

7:04 - 7:16 - write two complete pages.

7:16 - 7:18 - reread today's pages, - spell check, add several visual words.

7:18 - 7:20 - make notes for tomorrow's session.

As dedicated writer, you don't simply plop down and start spewing words. Review what you did yesterday, make a short outline for the today's pages, and then do the work. When you reread todays' pages, add a few descriptive words that heighten the emotion, conflict or setting.

Once a Week Review

Once a week, start your writing time with a brief overview. What scenes are you going to write? What is the week's plan? Take a glance at your scene cards, character descriptions and story description. This keeps you on track.

The process of completing a book is to follow the path you've created for yourself. Like a blueprint for a building, the story description is the IDEA of your book. Now you are in the construction phase, getting dirty, working daily and building something you can be proud of.

Chapter Six

Constant, Contained Conflict (CCC)

What do "Romeo and Juliet", "Twilight", "The Great Gatsby", "War and Peace", "Catch 22" and "Jurassic Park" have in common? They all contain Constant Contained Conflict.

Conflict drives stories forward and reveals character. What a character says is one thing, but what he **does**, especially under pressure, defines who he is. Conflict can also be used to describe the physical attributes of a person as well as the location and environment.

The contained portion of a conflict often involves emotional, political or financial ties, although physical containment is commonly used. Your story must have constant contained conflict if it is to maintain the reader's (and your) interest.

Different Levels of Conflict

There are large conflicts that will culminate in a dramatic showdown between the main character and the antagonist. There will be smaller ones, even between the good guys – which way should they go, fighting over a plan of attack, should they take the girl along, which weapon is best for the job, arguing about which trail to take.

There will also be conflicts within a character's personality - Should I do it? Should I tell her? Can I overcome my fear of snakes?

Without conflict, a story lies flat and lifeless. Even a biography or historical novel has internal and external struggles or it becomes a dry litany of details. Conflict brings a character's beliefs, joys, fears and loves to the surface where the audience can experience them.

Consider Shakespeare's "Romeo and Juliet". Everyone is in conflict and they are confined to family ties, relationships, loyalty, even to the city.

Don't be Boring - Create Conflict

If you are not a Shakespeare fan, think about the opposite situation – a twitter or Facebook poster who writes that they ate breakfast, saw a cute bird, went to a nice play and then retired to bed early. Totally boring. Why? There's no conflict.

What if that same individual ate a poisoned donut and nearly died, was attacked by a crazed falcon, was physically thrown out of Lincoln Center or was pulled out of bed and threatened with dismemberment by an angry, pregnant lover? You might be interested in finding out what was going on with this person.

Confinement intensifies everything. An explosion that detonates high in the air is often harmless. That same amount of energy restricted to the inside of a pipe or an enclosed room can be deadly. So it is with conflict. Confined conflict forces characters to deal with issues and each other. As a result, the reader is engaged.

How to Contain Conflict

One of the most common ways to contain conflict is with relationships. A wife will not leave because she doesn't want to lose custody of her kids. The daughter hates living at home but has nowhere to go. The police officer won't quit because his partner is in danger. High school teammates refuse to let the other down, and lie to protect their friend from going to jail.

Family, loyalty, love, commitment, friendship, debts and fear of reprisal can confine characters, forcing them to make decisions that reflect their limits, personality and morals.

Sometimes a writer uses walls to contain conflict. The protagonist could be trapped with an obnoxious friend or a dangerous enemy. Two lovers might argue about the best way to escape a collapsed building.

Not every conflict will be played at the same intensity. A low-level conflict about who is better at flipping pancakes will play differently than fighting over the possession of a key that will launch a nuclear missile.

The concept of constant contained conflict must be in the front of your mind as you plan your story. Each character and scene has to have elements of conflict. Some of these conflicts will be resolved within the scene. Others will carry over or resurface.

Conflict is a motivating force for a reader to continue and find "how it turns out."

Chapter Seven

Deadlines and Characters

Plot Plan

You already have a basic idea of what your book is about. In a short while you will have another exercise where you will create a cast of characters and outline scenes they will be in.

A goal without a deadline is a dream.

You need to set a final deadline. Writing a book is a time-consuming journey. You have to travel a little distance every day if you want to make it to the finish line.

I plan to finish the completed first draft of my book eight months from today, which will be on _____ (**date**).

Write this date in large letters on your calendar and in an obvious place in your life.

Characters and Scenes

Let's move on to the characters and scenes that will be in your book.

You are now going to create six balanced characters – three "good", three "bad", and one head bad guy, also known as "the antagonist."

Good Guys and Bad guys

The overall concept of the 3by3 Writing Method is a good guy/bad guy approach. If you look at any successful story, conflict is created by one character trying to achieve a goal and another trying to stop him.

Your "good guy" can be the worst villain in the world who is being blocked by his peers. In stories where everyone is a shade of evil, there is no actual "good guy." The 3by3 Writing Method uses the "good guy/bad guy" approach is to simplify the conflict between the opposing forces in your story.

Six Balanced Characters and One that's Demoted

Your book will require a minimum of seven major characters.

Each character will have an opposite, except the antagonist. If you do not balance characters, the story will be lopsided. Unbalanced stories result in a lack of constant contained conflict and often become boring.

The Antagonist is Demoted

In many stories, the traditional antagonist, the individual who blocks the main character's march toward his goal, is not revealed or confronted by the protagonist until much later in the story.

Even in stories where the antagonist participates, the antagonist is often directing his henchmen to do his dirty work until the climatic end when the protagonist and antagonist clash.

The 3by3 Writing Method makes a bold change in traditional storytelling method. Because the antagonist often works in the shadows, he has been removed from the conflict model in most situations.

We will call the assistant antagonist a traitor.

"Good Guys"

Main character (The Protagonist)

The Buddy & The Clown

"Bad Guys"

The Traitor (Assistant Antagonist)

The Enforcer & The Jerk

The Antagonist (Head Bad Guy)

The Balanced Characters

Main Character balances the Traitor

The Buddy balances the Enforcer

The Clown balances the Jerk

At the end

Main Character confronts the Antagonist

Each of the balanced characters square off. Occasionally they fight among themselves. As the protagonist approaches her goal, the opposing "bad" characters, with their own internal conflicts create more and more tension. Some switch sides. Some pretend to switch sides.

It often happens that the main character and the buddy are at odds. The Buddy knows there's trouble and tries to steer the main character from the oncoming danger, but the main character has a goal and is hell-bent to reach it.

In many "buddy movies" the main character teams up with the clown to provide wise-cracking banter during high energy scenes.

In romance stories, future lovers are often the protagonist and buddy, destined to fight for their right to be together.

In other stories the clown is tormented, threatened, or severely hurt by the enforcer and/or traitor to underscore the bad guys' nastiness and increase speed the main character's race to his goal.

On the following pages you will find fill-in-the-blank forms to clarify the story and your seven characters.

The Good Guys

Buddy Character Card

Character name

_____

Current or former occupation and age

_____

Unique physical aspect (scar, limp, odor, hair, harelip, flatulence)

_____

Why the buddy teamed up with the main character:

_____

Conflicting internal emotion

_____

Reason to dislike the antagonist

_____

Reason to dislike the main character

_____

Clown Character Card

Character name

_____

Current or former occupation and age

_____

Unique physical aspect (scar, limp, odor, hair, harelip, flatulence)

_____

Why the clown teamed up with the main character

_____

Conflicting internal emotion

_____

Reason to dislike the antagonist

_____

Reason to dislike the main character

_____

The Bad Guys

Traitor Character Card

Character name

Current or former occupation and age

Unique physical aspect (scar, limp, odor, hair, harelip, flatulence)

Why the traitor teamed up with the antagonist

Conflicting internal emotion

Reason to dislike the antagonist

Reason to dislike the main character

Enforcer Character Card

Character name

Current or former occupation and age

Unique physical aspect (scar, limp, odor, hair, harelip, flatulence)

Why the enforcer teamed up with the antagonist:

Conflicting internal emotion

Reason to dislike the antagonist

Reason to dislike the main character

Jerk Character Card

Character name

_____

Current or former occupation and age

_____

Unique physical aspect (scar, limp, odor, hair, harelip, flatulence)

_____

Why the jerk teamed up with the antagonist

_____

Conflicting internal emotion

_____

Reason to dislike the antagonist

_____

Reason to dislike the main character

_____

Head Bad Guy/Antagonist Character Card

Character name

_____

Current or former occupation and age

_____

Unique physical aspect (scar, limp, odor, hair, harelip, flatulence)

_____

Reason to dislike the main character

_____

Source of his power

_____

Major weakness

_____

Why is the antagonist trying to stop the protagonist from achieving his/her goal?

_____

What is the antagonist's conflicting internal emotion?

_____

MAIN CAST LIST

GOOD GUYS

Main character: _____

Buddy: _____

Clown: _____

BAD GUYS

Traitor: _____

Enforcer: _____

Jerk: _____

THE "HEAD BAD GUY"/ANTAGONIST:

_____

You now have a story and a cast. Only a few more details to work out and then the writing begins.

Chapter Eight

Developing Scenes

Next up is filling in the scene forms will prepare you for writing the first draft of your book. Do not fill in the book order number until you have created all the necessary scenes, then you can decide which scene goes where. Leave the last scene form blank. Save it as an extra that you can copy or use for reference.

THE BOOK OF SCENES

Once you have at least fifteen scenes prepared you can go to your writing space, get comfortable and create a few pages. If you have more than fifteen scenes to describe, make copies of the extra scene form and add these scenes to your list before starting.

You also might consider making photocopies of your story description, scene forms, deadline, writing schedule and character descriptions. Put these into a three ring binder that you keep near your writing space for quick reference.

Each scene form represents a chapter, so at the start of your writing you will have at least fifteen chapters you can develop.

Scenes not in the Book

You say, "But the scene where my main character has his heart broken won't be in the book."

Complete a scene form for that event so you know all the details that occur. When you are done with the other scenes within your story, incorporate this event somewhere through the use of dialogue, a flashback, or a character's thoughts about their past.

Listed below are scenes that could be used in your story. The most effective scene is one that starts off one way and ends with the real purpose revealed. During that discovery, more of the plot is revealed.

Required Scenes

Protagonist's internal conflict	Trigger event
Protagonist's initial emotional status	Protagonist chooses his goal
Protagonist's intensified emotion	Protagonist's final action
Final consequence	Revelation
Antagonist faces the Protagonist	

Scene Suggestions

Protagonist meets the antagonist	The traitor's internal conflict
The clown's internal conflict	Enforcer joins the antagonist
Clown joins the protagonist	Protagonist gets a nick name
Traitor joins the antagonist	The 1st death or injury
Protagonist forgives the enforcer.	Buddy joins the Protagonist
Why the enforcer hates the protagonist	
How the buddy joined the protagonist	

The reason for all this preparation is to get you to understand your story in some detail. When you reach that difficult area in the middle of your book, you'll know what scenes to write.

Characters' Physical Description

Conflicts and descriptive writing will reveal your character's physical appearance. For instance, you don't have go into great detail if a person is confined to a wheelchair. All you have to do is explain how that person struggles to navigate a damaged handicapped ramp, how they get into the passenger seat of a car, or describe another character's realization that their childhood friend cannot walk.

A character's unique physical characteristic can reveal her inner conflict, or motivation. The Traitor might hate the main character because she blames him for the facial scar that ruined modeling career.

An eye patch, an arm in a sling, a missing finger, a limp, that bad haircut, her mismatched clothing or an odd mode of transportation can add to a character's distinctiveness and their history.

Make notes on the form about settings, appearances, aspects of the location, weather, time of day, a character's footwear, clothing or favorite food.

Basic Elements of a Scene

Each scene should have at least two purposes – the initial reason and the revealed reason. A scene with no purpose does not belong anywhere in your story.

A well-developed scene will begin heading in a specific direction – like a guy is going to break up with his girlfriend. As the action and dialogue progress, another issue will be revealed - that she's been dating two other men; his best friend and his boss.

Each of the seven major characters should have an unstated internal conflict that can be used within the scene. This could be a problem that's been used before, like the killer hates getting blood on her.

In other cases the conflict could be a new issue. Perhaps the character becomes uncontrollably angry when a man pats her on the head, indicating a problem to be revealed later - that she hates being treated like a child, especially by men who think they're superior to women.

With each character having an internal and external conflict, you can pick the ones you want to explore in a particular scene. Not every conflict will be resolved, but one or two can be exploited in a scene and used to create drama.

You might take a few pages to explain why the enforcer is so intent on hurting the protagonist or why the clown is afraid of forming permanent relationships.

SCENE EXAMPLE

On the next page is an example of a completed scene form. The nice thing about the 3by3 Writing Method is that these scene and character descriptions are not carved stone. They are designed so the details of a character's physical and emotional situations are exposed.

SCENE TITLE - <u>Dart Scene</u>

Characters in the scene: – Jack (protagonist), Mary (traitor), Quint (buddy).

Purpose of scene - Quint wants to show his friend, Jack, that Mary has a terrible temper and that Quint might be in danger.

Revealed purpose(s) of the scene - Mary is a lesbian trying to get pregnant and hates men.

External conflict(s) – Jack likes Mary a lot but doesn't totally trust her. He senses something is wrong. Quint is a playboy and is sleeping with Mary's roommate.

Internal conflict(s) – Jack was emotionally damaged by a previous one-night stand does not trust bar hookups. Mary is using Jack to get pregnant. Quint has caused issues with Jack's previous relationships.

One resolution that occurs in the scene – Jack decides Mary is more important than Quint.

How the remaining conflicts are carried forward (or resolved) – Quint tells Jack that Mary might be gay because she's been in a gay bar. Jack remembers that his former one-night stand started at a bar and that relationship broke his heart.

What happens at the beginning of the scene? - Quint, Jack and Mary are playing darts in a bar. Quint tries to provoke Mary.

What happens at the end of the scene? - Jack argues with Quint and damages his relationship with Quint.

There are a number of ways this scene could be played. The game could be pool instead of darts. The competition could become fierce. Jack could threaten quint with darts or a pool cue. Mary's roommate could show up to create tension.

SCENE CARD #1

STORY ORDER #_____   BOOK ORDER #_____
(The way the story happens.)   (Order scene occurs in the book. Use pencil.)

SCENE TITLE _____

Main characters in the scene: _____ _____

_____ _____   _____

Initial purpose of the scene: _____

_____

(Every scene must have a reason to be in the book.)

Revealed purpose of scene: _____

_____

External conflict(s) _____

_____

Internal conflict(s)_____

_____

One resolution that occurs in the scene:_____ _____

_____

How the remaining conflicts are carried forward (or resolved)

_____

What happens at the beginning of the scene? _____

_____

(This is the action that occurs.)

What happens at the end of the scene? _____

_____

There should be conflict in every scene and behind every character's action.

SCENE CARD #2

STORY ORDER   #____   BOOK ORDER #_____
(The way the story happens.)   (Order scene occurs in the book. Use pencil.)

SCENE TITLE _____

Main characters in the scene: _____ _____

_____ _____   _____

Initial purpose of the scene: _____

_____

(Every scene must have a reason to be in the book.)

Revealed purpose of scene: _____

_____

External conflict(s) _____

_____

Internal conflict(s)_____

_____

One resolution that occurs in the scene:_____ _____

_____

How the remaining conflicts are carried forward (or resolved)

_____

What happens at the beginning of the scene? _____

_____

(This is the action that occurs.)

What happens at the end of the scene? _____

_____

There should be conflict in every scene and behind every character's action.

SCENE CARD #3

STORY ORDER   #_____   BOOK ORDER #_____
(The way the story happens.)   (Order scene occurs in the book. Use pencil.)

SCENE TITLE _____

Main characters in the scene: _____ _____

_____ _____   _____

Initial purpose of the scene: _____

_____

(Every scene must have a reason to be in the book.)

Revealed purpose of scene: _____

_____

External conflict(s) _____

_____

Internal conflict(s)_____

_____

One resolution that occurs in the scene:_____ _____

_____

How the remaining conflicts are carried forward (or resolved)

_____

What happens at the beginning of the scene? _____

_____

(This is the action that occurs.)

What happens at the end of the scene? _____

_____

There should be conflict in every scene and behind every character's action.

SCENE CARD #4

STORY ORDER   #____   BOOK ORDER #_____
(The way the story happens.)   (Order scene occurs in the book. Use pencil.)

SCENE TITLE _____

Main characters in the scene: _____ _____

_____ _____   _____

Initial purpose of the scene: _____

_____

(Every scene must have a reason to be in the book.)

Revealed purpose of scene: _____

_____

External conflict(s) _____

_____

Internal conflict(s)_____

_____

One resolution that occurs in the scene:_____ _____

_____

How the remaining conflicts are carried forward (or resolved)

_____

What happens at the beginning of the scene? _____

_____

(This is the action that occurs.)

What happens at the end of the scene? _____

_____

There should be conflict in every scene and behind every character's action.

SCENE CARD #5

STORY ORDER   #____   BOOK ORDER #_____
(The way the story happens.)   (Order scene occurs in the book. Use pencil.)

SCENE TITLE _____

Main characters in the scene: _____ _____

_____ _____   _____

Initial purpose of the scene: _____

_____

(Every scene must have a reason to be in the book.)

Revealed purpose of scene: _____

_____

External conflict(s) _____

_____

Internal conflict(s)_____

_____

One resolution that occurs in the scene:_____ _____

_____

How the remaining conflicts are carried forward (or resolved)

_____

What happens at the beginning of the scene? _____

_____

(This is the action that occurs.)

What happens at the end of the scene? _____

_____

There should be conflict in every scene and behind every character's action.

SCENE CARD #6

STORY ORDER #____   BOOK ORDER #_____
(The way the story happens.)   (Order scene occurs in the book. Use pencil.)

SCENE TITLE _____

Main characters in the scene: _____ _____

_____ _____   _____

Initial purpose of the scene: _____

_____

(Every scene must have a reason to be in the book.)

Revealed purpose of scene: _____

_____

External conflict(s) _____

_____

Internal conflict(s)_____

_____

One resolution that occurs in the scene:_____ _____

_____

How the remaining conflicts are carried forward (or resolved)

_____

What happens at the beginning of the scene? _____

_____

(This is the action that occurs.)

What happens at the end of the scene? _____

_____

There should be conflict in every scene and behind every character's action.

SCENE CARD #7

STORY ORDER   #_____   BOOK ORDER #_____
(The way the story happens.)   (Order scene occurs in the book. Use pencil.)

SCENE TITLE _____

Main characters in the scene: _____ _____

_____ _____   _____

Initial purpose of the scene: _____

_____

(Every scene must have a reason to be in the book.)

Revealed purpose of scene: _____

_____

External conflict(s) _____

_____

Internal conflict(s)_____

_____

One resolution that occurs in the scene:_____ _____

_____

How the remaining conflicts are carried forward (or resolved)

_____

What happens at the beginning of the scene? _____

_____

(This is the action that occurs.)

What happens at the end of the scene? _____

_____

There should be conflict in every scene and behind every character's action.

SCENE CARD #8

STORY ORDER   #_____   BOOK ORDER #_____
(The way the story happens.)   (Order scene occurs in the book. Use pencil.)

SCENE TITLE _____

Main characters in the scene: _____ _____

_____ _____   _____

Initial purpose of the scene: _____

_____

(Every scene must have a reason to be in the book.)

Revealed purpose of scene: _____

_____

External conflict(s) _____

_____

Internal conflict(s)_____

_____

One resolution that occurs in the scene:_____ _____

_____

How the remaining conflicts are carried forward (or resolved)

_____

What happens at the beginning of the scene? _____

_____

(This is the action that occurs.)

What happens at the end of the scene? _____

_____

There should be conflict in every scene and behind every character's action.

SCENE CARD #9

STORY ORDER   #_____   BOOK ORDER #_____
(The way the story happens.)   (Order scene occurs in the book. Use pencil.)

SCENE TITLE _____

Main characters in the scene: _____ _____

_____ _____   _____

Initial purpose of the scene: _____

_____

(Every scene must have a reason to be in the book.)

Revealed purpose of scene: _____

_____

External conflict(s) _____

_____

Internal conflict(s)_____

_____

One resolution that occurs in the scene:_____ _____

_____

How the remaining conflicts are carried forward (or resolved)

_____

What happens at the beginning of the scene? _____

_____

(This is the action that occurs.)

What happens at the end of the scene? _____

_____

There should be conflict in every scene and behind every character's action.

SCENE CARD #10

STORY ORDER   #____   BOOK ORDER #_____
(The way the story happens.)   (Order scene occurs in the book. Use pencil.)

SCENE TITLE _____

Main characters in the scene: _____ _____

_____ _____   _____

Initial purpose of the scene: _____

_____

(Every scene must have a reason to be in the book.)

Revealed purpose of scene: _____

_____

External conflict(s) _____

_____

Internal conflict(s)_____

_____

One resolution that occurs in the scene:_____ _____

_____

How the remaining conflicts are carried forward (or resolved)

_____

What happens at the beginning of the scene? _____

_____

(This is the action that occurs.)

What happens at the end of the scene? _____ ____

_____

There should be conflict in every scene and behind every character's action.

SCENE CARD #11

STORY ORDER   #_____   BOOK ORDER #_____
(The way the story happens.)   (Order scene occurs in the book. Use pencil.)

SCENE TITLE _____

Main characters in the scene: _____ _____

_____ _____   _____

Initial purpose of the scene: _____

_____

(Every scene must have a reason to be in the book.)

Revealed purpose of scene: _____

_____

External conflict(s) _____

_____

Internal conflict(s)_____

_____

One resolution that occurs in the scene:_____ _____

_____

How the remaining conflicts are carried forward (or resolved)

_____

What happens at the beginning of the scene? _____

_____

(This is the action that occurs.)

What happens at the end of the scene? _____

_____

There should be conflict in every scene and behind every character's action.

SCENE CARD #12

STORY ORDER   #____   BOOK ORDER #_____
(The way the story happens.)   (Order scene occurs in the book. Use pencil.)

SCENE TITLE _____

Main characters in the scene: _____ _____

____ _____   _____

Initial purpose of the scene: _____

_____

(Every scene must have a reason to be in the book.)

Revealed purpose of scene: _____

_____

External conflict(s) _____

_____

Internal conflict(s)_____

_____

One resolution that occurs in the scene:_____ _____

_____

How the remaining conflicts are carried forward (or resolved)

_____

What happens at the beginning of the scene? _____

_____

(This is the action that occurs.)

What happens at the end of the scene? _____

_____

There should be conflict in every scene and behind every character's action.

SCENE CARD #13

STORY ORDER   #____   BOOK ORDER #_____
(The way the story happens.)   (Order scene occurs in the book. Use pencil.)

SCENE TITLE _____

Main characters in the scene: _____ _____

_____ _____   _____

Initial purpose of the scene: _____

_____

(Every scene must have a reason to be in the book.)

Revealed purpose of scene: _____

_____

External conflict(s) _____

_____

Internal conflict(s)_____

_____

One resolution that occurs in the scene:_____ _____

_____

How the remaining conflicts are carried forward (or resolved)

_____

What happens at the beginning of the scene? _____

_____

(This is the action that occurs.)

What happens at the end of the scene? _____

_____

There should be conflict in every scene and behind every character's action.

SCENE CARD #14

STORY ORDER   #_____   BOOK ORDER #_____
(The way the story happens.)   (Order scene occurs in the book. Use pencil.)

SCENE TITLE _____

Main characters in the scene: _____ _____

_____ _____   _____

Initial purpose of the scene: _____

_____

(Every scene must have a reason to be in the book.)

Revealed purpose of scene: _____

_____

External conflict(s) _____

_____

Internal conflict(s)_____

_____

One resolution that occurs in the scene:_____ _____

_____

How the remaining conflicts are carried forward (or resolved)

_____

What happens at the beginning of the scene? _____

_____

(This is the action that occurs.)

What happens at the end of the scene? _____

_____

There should be conflict in every scene and behind every character's action.

SCENE CARD #15

STORY ORDER   #_____   BOOK ORDER #_____
(The way the story happens.)   (Order scene occurs in the book. Use pencil.)

SCENE TITLE _____

Main characters in the scene: _____ _____

_____ _____   _____

Initial purpose of the scene: _____

_____

(Every scene must have a reason to be in the book.)

Revealed purpose of scene: _____

_____

External conflict(s) _____

_____

Internal conflict(s)_____

_____

One resolution that occurs in the scene:_____ _____

_____

How the remaining conflicts are carried forward (or resolved)

_____

What happens at the beginning of the scene? _____

_____

(This is the action that occurs.)

What happens at the end of the scene? _____

_____

There should be conflict in every scene and behind every character's action.

SCENE CARD - (SAVE FOR REFERENCE)

STORY ORDER   #_____   BOOK ORDER #_____
(The way the story happens.)   (Order scene occurs in the book. Use pencil.)

SCENE TITLE _____

Main characters in the scene: _____ _____

_____ _____   _____

Initial purpose of the scene: _____

_____

(Every scene must have a reason to be in the book.)

Revealed purpose of scene: _____

_____

External conflict(s) _____

_____

Internal conflict(s)_____

_____

One resolution that occurs in the scene:_____ _____

_____

How the remaining conflicts are carried forward (or resolved)

_____

What happens at the beginning of the scene? _____

_____

(This is the action that occurs.)

What happens at the end of the scene? _____

_____

There should be conflict in every scene and behind every character's action.

Chapter Nine

The First Draft

It is time to get a lot of words on the page. If you are a serious writer, you NEED a computer and a word processor. Microsoft's Word is a powerful program. Microsoft's Works is a similar writing program. There is a free office suite available online called Open Office that program contains a potent word processor. You can download free it at openoffice.org. Choose your own writing software and become familiar with whichever program you use.

File creation

In order to keep your writing files separate from others, you will need to start a new computer folder with the name of your book. It could be on the desktop or on your hard drive.

After you create a folder with the name of your book, open your word processor and save a file with the name of your book and the number 1 after it (Jaws 1) and save these files in your novel folder.

You will be saving multiple copies of your partially completed manuscript.

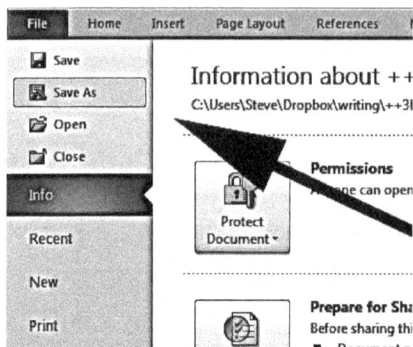

Each time you save a new version of your file, you will be using the "save as" command and an incremental number (Jaws 1... Jaws 2... Jaws 3). An alternative would be to use the current date (Jaws May 15 2012.... Jaws June 01 2012... Jaws June 15 2012 etc.)

You should make it a habit to save your book with a new version number at least every two weeks.

If you are writing your book longhand, you need to begin your search for someone to type your book into a computer for later revisions.

Formatting the Manuscript

The following paragraphs show how to format a manuscript in Windows MS Word 2010. Here are the basic requirements.

> One inch margins on all sides except the top, which is 1.3 inches to allow room for your header.

> Paragraphs are to be double-spaced.

> The page number, title and last name go in the left side header at the top of the page.

Start each chapter on a new page, with the title one-third of the way down

Page Setup

Go to the top tab in your Microsoft Word 2010 program and find the heading labeled "Page Layout." On the bottom of the section is a label "Page Setup" and to the right of this label is a little arrow pointing down. Click on that and a dialogue box will appear.

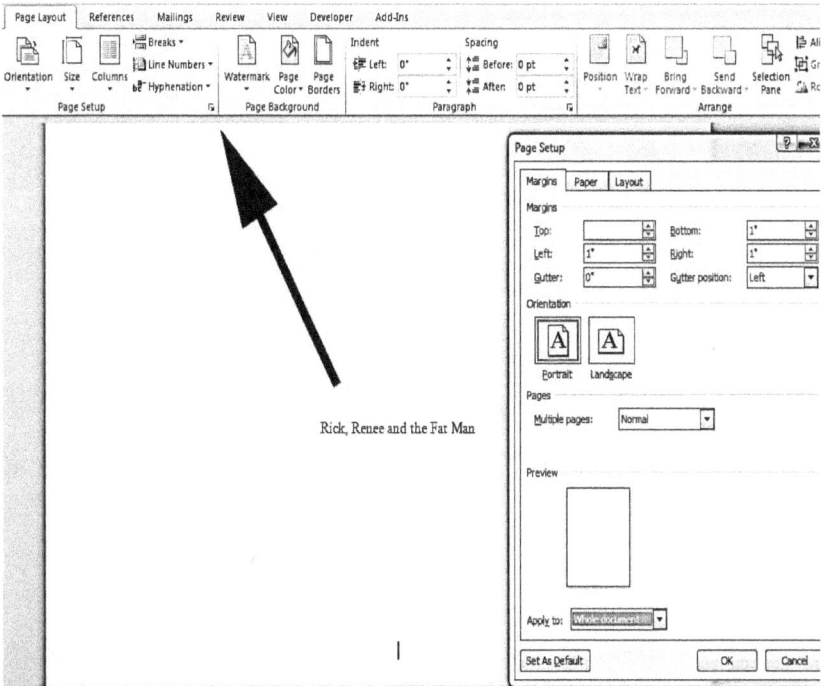

Here are the settings you want:

Margins - top 1.3" all others 1"   **Gutter -** 0"

Gutter position - left   **Orientation -** portrait

Multiple pages – normal   **Apply to** – whole document.

Paragraph Setup

If you have already started writing your book, select "CTRL" and the letter "A". This will select the entire file.

Go to the top section labeled "Home" and then go to the section marked "Paragraph," directly under the heading called "View". There is a little down-pointing arrow to the right of the word "Paragraph." Click on that to bring up the dialogue box. Clicking on the "Indents and Spacing" tab.

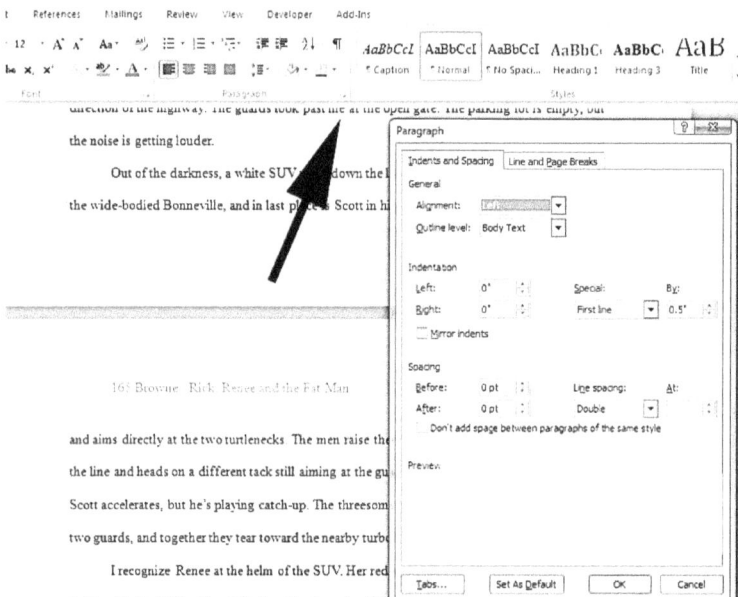

Here are the settings.

Alignment: "left"

Outline level: "Body Text"

Indentation: left 0" right 0"

Special: first line at .5"

Space before and after: 0"

Line spacing: double.

At the top of the dialogue box, **select "Line and Page Breaks"**

Deselect line orphan and window control, all others, leave unchecked

Exit the dialogue box by checking "ok" at the bottom of the page.

That should format the entire manuscript. To make sure every future paragraph starts with these settings, go to the "Home" tab, then click on the small arrow to the right of "Paragraph" again and click the "Set as Default" and when the next box appears, select "This Document Only".

Now, select "CTRL" and the letter "A" once more. Go to the "home" tab at top left make the font Times New Roman, and make the font size 12.

Paragraph Styles Easy Formatting

An alternative way to keep paragraphs in the same format is to adjust the paragraph style located in the center of MS Word 2010's top section under the "Home" tab.

There is a style called "normal." If you right-click on it, there is a section called "Modify". Select this.

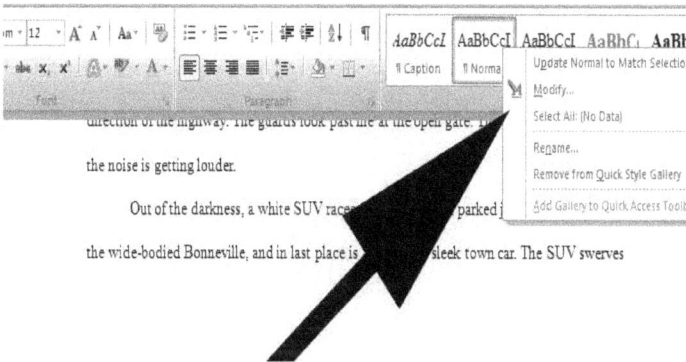

A new dialogue box will appear. In the center of this box, make sure your font is Times New Roman or Courier with a font size of twelve points.

At the bottom left of the dialogue box is a tab for "Format". Select Format, then Paragraph.

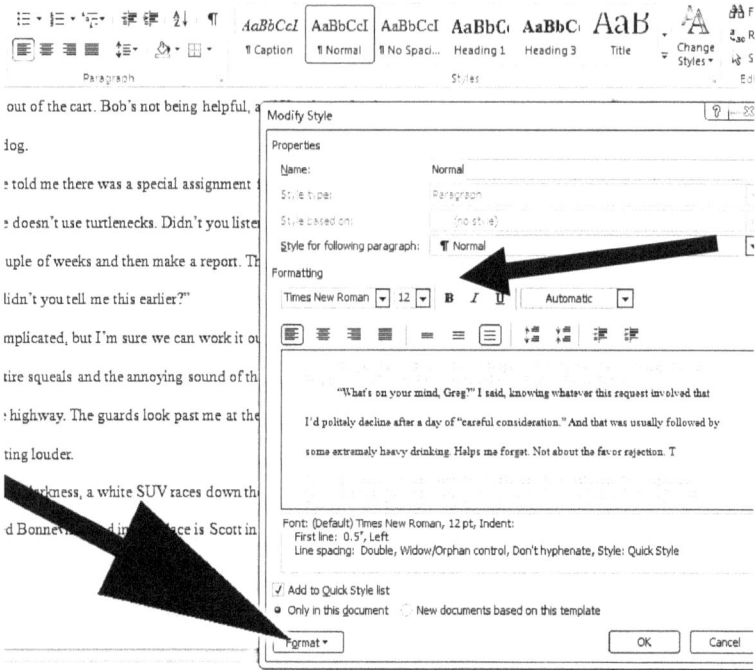

Here are the settings.

Alignment: "left" **Outline level** - "Body Text"

Indentation: left 0" right 0" **Special** - first line at .5"

Space before and after: 0" **Line spacing**: double.

At the top of the dialogue box, select **"Line and Page Breaks"**

Deselect line orphan and window control, all others, leave unchecked

Exit the **paragraph** dialogue box by checking "ok" at the bottom of the page.

Exit the style dialogue box by checking "ok" at the bottom of the page.

Select "CTRL" and the letter "A", then click on the normal style and the entire file will be formatted to that specific paragraph style. You will have to work a little on your chapter headings but the body of the text format is done.

One click on **Normal** in the style gallery any place within a paragraph will force it into the "normal" style.

Also every new paragraph will be created in the "normal" style.

Formatting the Header

Go to top tab labeled "Insert." Look along the bottom labels and you will see "Header & Footer" to the right of center. Click on page number, top of page, and then select page number one. This will insert the page number into your manuscript.

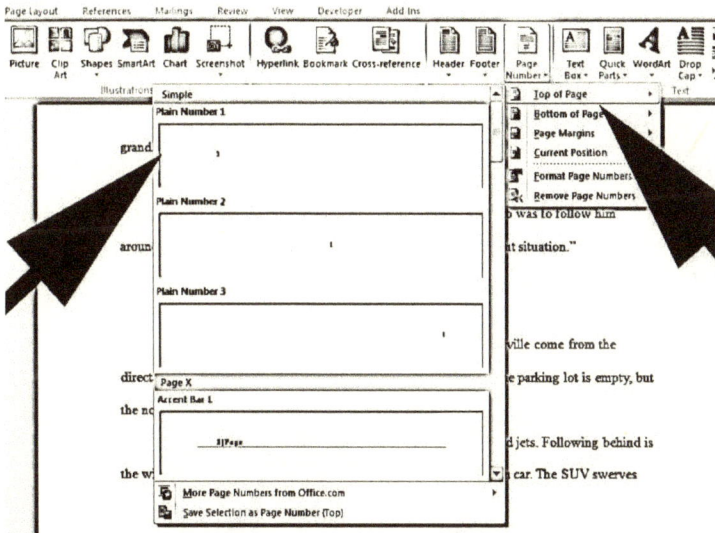

Click to the right of the page number and, then type your last name then "/", then the title of your book in the header.

Double left click on the manuscript text to exit the header.

Starting Chapters

To begin your manuscript hit enter a few times and type "Chapter One" or your chapter title. One more "enter" and this is where you start your book.

When you want to start a new chapter on a new page, go to the top tab labeled "Insert," and on the left is an icon called "Page Break." Select that, go one-third down the page, type "Chapter Two" and then start your second chapter.

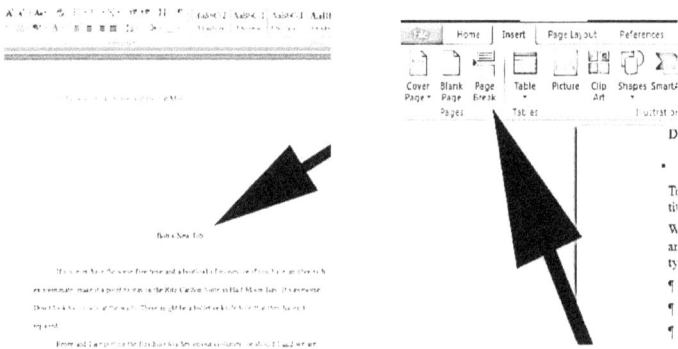

First Words

Writing the first words of your book can be a challenge. Even with scenes planned and knowing your main character's final goal, staring at that blank screen can be intimidating. Remember you are not working on the next great American novel. It's the first draft of a book.

If you do not know where to start, below is a helpful first sentence. The two underlines are for your main character's first and last name.

_____ _____ was heading for trouble. He didn't know it at the time, but….. (Okay, your turn.)

Build Paragraphs with Images

Here are a few words of advice that have wormed their way into my breezy second-story porch where I write to the sounds of chirping sparrows and the occasional roar of a Harley-Davidson motorcycle.

A descriptive paragraph is peppered with words that convey images of visuals, smells, and the scene's environment. A dead-of-winter New England forest and looks, sounds, smells and, feels very different from a deserted Hollywood Boulevard at 5 a.m. on a mid-summer's weekday.

It only takes a few well-placed descriptions; greasy hands, spotless loafers, bushy eyebrows, to bring your sentences and paragraphs to life. Use words that matter, not necessarily words you know.

With dialogue, the words chosen tell the reader who is talking and how they feel about the person they are talking to. Even a greeting: Hey chump, Lover girl, Butt face, Honey...can convey a specific relationship and intent.

The attribute - "he mumbled under his vodka-laced breath," or "he spat on the mugger's soiled shoes," helps create an image in the readers' mind.

"He shaded his blue eyes from the bright sunlight." "She noticed his strong unshaven chin." "His tweed jacket looked out of place in the seedy bar." These are examples of how to describe your characters without listing their looks or appearance.

Reading Other's Works Can Show You the Way

To understand the details of writing it is a good idea to read books of the same type as yours. Published novels are examples of the type of books that consumers read, and the ones that publishers buy.

When you like the style of a particular writer, examine what they did with their words. There's always something to learn from reading.

Your Book Can be That Good

It is important to remember that you are **not** writing a Nobel-winning tour de force. The masterpiece shows up in rewrites, when your subconscious kicks in and those great ideas that came to you during the creative process are carefully introduced into the revised draft.

Make notes as these ideas come forward, but don't let a brief moment of misplaced inspiration stop your writing momentum.

At the end of each session, reread your work, fix the glaring errors, and clean up any misspellings. Make notes for the next day's session, and save the file.

USEFUL MS Word Short Cuts

Some of the following shortcuts are Windows-based and others are specific to MSWord, but I'll leave you to figure alternatives out if you are a MAC/Apple user.

> Control/shift/end – highlights from your cursor to the end of the file
>
> Control/shift/home – highlights from your cursor to the top of the file
>
> Double click highlights a word
>
> Triple click highlights a paragraph
>
> F7 is spell check
>
> Control/H is "Search and Replace
>
> Control/F is Find
>
> Control/A is Select All
>
> Right click on a misspelled word will offer correct spelling, as well as several formatting options and an option to view synonyms.

Undo, Redo and Bookmarks

At the top left of MSWord 2010 are several blue icons – one is **Undo**. One is **Redo** or Put back if you hit delete too many times. These icons are the same as "CTRL plus Z" (undo), which is the opposite of "CTRL plus Y" (redo).

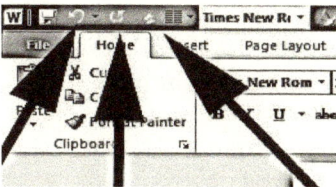

There is also a little blue flag at the top left of MS Word. This is a **bookmark**. You can click on this icon and a dialog box will appear. You can type in a bookmark and "add" it to the manuscript.

This puts a place marker in your test. You cannot use spaces in the bookmark description, but you can label the book mark as "chapter_one" and then you can jump around your novel by selecting this flag and clicking on one of labels in the bookmark.

Double Spaces after a Sentence

The days of double spacing after a period have passed. However, for some people, it is a habit hard to forget. "CTRL/H" enables "Find and Replace." Search for period, and then two spaces, replace with period and one space. You can select "Change All." This is a quick way to eliminate all double spaces after a period.

Search and Replace Disasters

The Search and Replace function can cause trouble throughout your manuscript if you are not careful. Replacing the name "Rick" can affect other words like "Herrick" or "brick" or "stricken." Make sure you put a space before and after any name change. You can also select "whole words only."

Going Backwards and Reworking

After you have written for a week or two, do you head back and polish those pages? Ah...no.

Even if your uncle is a wealthy New York publisher, you need to keep moving forward and finish your draft. Do not back up.

Start each week with the same determination as the first. Only rewrite the previous day's work. If there's something to fix or change, put that reminder into a notebook and keep writing in your current location. Don't be jumping all around your manuscript making repairs.

If you follow your plan and stay true to your dedicated time, you will have a completed rough draft between six months and nine months, perhaps sooner.

You will have notes for the next pass and lots of ideas that came to mind during the creation of your first draft. Keep on your path. Work your main character's journey all the way to the end of the first draft.

The reason why you do not back up is there will be more notes that come to mind as you progress. You need to complete the draft to see how your story takes shape. Constantly backing up is not productive and it distracts from the story telling process.

When to Back Up and Start from the Beginning

When do you start over? When the book you began no longer exists: the plot has changed and the main character has changed, the supporting characters have changed. Then you will have to open a new file and start the entire process over. This is an entirely new book.

Try to avoid this drastic measure. The best idea is to finish the current draft, take a break for at least two weeks then reread the book from beginning to end. If you spent time at the start of your book with a plan, you probably have a very good story, but like all first drafts, it needs help, revision and reworking.

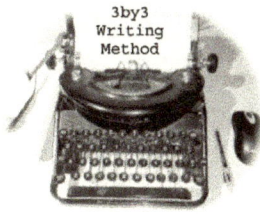

Chapter Ten

More Writing Issues

There are days when your paragraphs sing and dance. And there are days when your words fall flat and lifeless. Experiencing an off day is no reason to break stride. Boring paragraphs often contain elements of an excellent scene. They just aren't perfect.

Remember, no one judges how long it takes to write a book; they care only about the result.

Letting Family or Friends Read Early Drafts

Writers make up lots of stuff, but when writers use real people's names and personality traits trouble can occur. If you let friends or family read an early draft, they could become upset over nothing because that character or unique physical trait could be eliminated.

If do you use a friend or family member as a basis for one of your undesirable characters, be prepared for a bump in your relationship. Trying to explain why your best friend is portrayed as a sniveling, backstabbing hunchback is not always easy.

An alternative idea would be to make her the clever, all-powerful heroine.

Never use the real name of anyone you know. One trick to hiding a personal trait is to switch the gender. Take that overly loud male cousin and make that character a woman.

Inspiration Versus Planned Writing

You're sitting in your writing spot and suddenly, out of nowhere, a flood of words, conflicts, scenes and ideas come pouring into your mind. These are rare moments of creativity that must be captured.

If this special time does materialize and it is about the **current project,** open a new file (control N in MS Word).

If this idea is about another book or story idea, read the next section about wanting to write a different book.

There's usually no time to rewrite, correct spelling, or fix grammar during these intense, usually brief, stretches of creativity. Write as fast as you can. Make your notes understandable and indicate which dialogue is for which character. Save this file on your desktop with a name you will quickly recognize.

The long run of writing a novel allows for time to clean up ideas, scenes and dialogue that are created during an inspired speed writing session. It isn't every day that we are blessed with a portal to unique thoughts and dialogue, so it is a good plan to get those concepts written down and then return to your daily routine.

Review this file when you reread your notes for the second draft. It is important to get a complete first draft before heading back to the start of your story.

Wanting to write a different book

You're working on your middle chapters. You aren't feeling that initial excitement and this is not the drama-filled ending you really want to write.

Then it hits you. This is such a great idea! It's a story about a masked skydiver who's an international secret agent/wine connoisseur who falls in love with a pacifist librarian who hates drama, drinkers and airplanes.

This is a trick. A new book seems exciting because it's fresh and not completely thought out. If you really like the concept, write it down (not during your writing time) and file it for another time when you're searching for a new idea. Do not stop writing your current book. This type of distraction will always show up when the writing gets challenging. Don't fall for it.

Antidote for the Solitary Writer's Life

Even though writers work alone, they enjoy knowing that others share the same frustrations, elations and triumphs. The 3by3 Writing Method encourages networking. This pertains not only to gaining access to agents and publishers, but also for getting tips and suggestions from fellow writers.

Consider a social group based around the writing experiences or sharing experiences and ideas. Experienced authors enjoy sharing their tips and secrets, as well as hearing reactions to their own writing.

It is a good idea to join a critique or social group and see what they are about. Critique groups can provide technical help as well as motivation.

Many of these gatherings can be found online, including the popular Meetup.com website. Remember, joining a group is not a lifetime commitment.

Critique Groups

When you participate in a critique group, review your submission numerous times before handing it over, otherwise the response you receive might be hard to take. Read your pages out loud before you give them to someone. Some critique groups have the author read their pages aloud during the session.

Constantly Rewriting the First Three Chapters

Many beginning writers rewrite the first three to five chapters of their book over and over. There are a few reasons for this.

1 – The enthusiastic writer had a "great idea," but did not plan the middle or end of the book.

2 – The writer is blocked and keeps rewriting the stuff he knows, hoping to have some kind of inspiration that will give him the next step in their story.

3 – See number one.

The Writing Conference Dilemma

Every year there are scores of writing conferences that take place across the country. There are conferences for every style of writing and they occur at different times of the year. Do you attend a conference if you are midway through a book?

Without a finished manuscript, you certainly shouldn't approach professional agents to read your material, but making contacts, discovering what your craft is all about, can be a reasonable goal at a conference.

Attending a writer's conference can cost between $500 to $3500, depending on the price of the event, transportation, lodging, food, additional pitch/query/writing sessions and professional advice.

Conferences are an excellent way to connect with publishers, agents, and other writers.

If you have a completed first draft then a writing conference would be an excellent investment to meet other writers and learn what is needed when you are ready to submit your book to agents and publishers.

Talking about your plot to others

Sometimes you need to hash out specific details or go over your story description with a fellow writer, friend or partner. With hundreds of thousands of books published yearly, someone wrote a story similar to yours, probably this year, so your idea is not totally unique.

However, your vision will be a special one. The best bet is to talk about your ideas and concepts in general terms. Keep the details of your one-eyed villain with the poison-tipped knitting needle to yourself.

If you do share your ideas, do it with the few people you trust. Make sure they understand not to tell <u>anyone</u> your ideas or story plot.

Don't go to a bar and describe your entire story to see if people like it. Finish your book, and then tell everyone what your book is about while handing out business cards so they can **buy** it.

Protect Your Drafts

Every two weeks a new version of your book should be saved.

It is also a good idea to protect your files somewhere other than your computer. This can be done by transferring your files to a backup drive or thumb drive. You can also use an online storage area like Google Docs or Dropbox.

Dropbox (Dropbox.com) offers a solution for protecting your writing, with enough free storage to keep copies of your multiple versions on their drives in addition to your computers' hard drive.

Consider looking into Dropbox as a protection against computer failure. It automatically uploads your files if you change them. You can access these files from any computer with your password. It is a great idea for protecting your many months of hard work. Most of your word files will "fit" in their free space.

Keeping the Faith

No one throws 80,000 to 100,000 words into a computer and miraculously comes up with a bestseller. No one writes one version of a book and never changes a word, plot, or character description.

Have faith in yourself. Your plot and first draft might not be as wonderful as you'd like. It's okay. Revisions will bring your story to life.

Drinking and Writing

Drinking can be fun. Writing can be fun. Put them together and you have a recipe for disaster. The list of writers who either failed or didn't finish anything because of their drinking is long and sad.

The 3by3 Writing Method does not discourage drinking and writing. However, writing a book is a difficult job. Drinking can make it harder, considering that alcohol is a depressant. Writers write. Drinkers drink. Drunken writers do not often succeed.

How Long Does it Take?

Meeting with critique groups, consulting with mentors, and carefully crafting revisions take time. Work steadily and enjoy the process. After all, when you are done you'll be writing another book, so what's the rush?

Social Outings Provide Inspiration

Your characters live and work in shops, on trains, in restaurants and in the streets. Get your nails done and look around. Go to the local bus station or the airport. Watch how people interact with each other and with strangers. Have dinner with your friends and listen to the conversation change as the wine is consumed. Your canvas is outside your writing place.

Smells and Textures

A writer uses all her tools to create an **emotional** experience. Hair and eye color are important, but a person's hands tell another story. The texture of someone's clothes, even bathroom wallpaper can reveal a Martha Stewart lifestyle or one of chipped paint and smells that require a special description.

It is a good idea to mentally pause while writing a scene and look around in your mind's eye. That crack in the ceiling and the old spiderweb in the corner and the lack of any electrical outlets are clues as to where you are and the environment your character is trying to enter, or escape from. Don't imagine it; write it.

Exercise Stimulates Creativity

You write with your conscious mind, but you create in conjunction with your subconscious. One of the ways this creative teamwork can be encouraged is through exercise. There is a threshold that is crossed even during mild exercise, like walking, where the conscious mind is so occupied with the physical process that the subconscious is allowed temporary access. Great ideas can occur during this time.

It is also a good idea to keep a notepad at your bedside. A late-night dream will not stay in your memory until morning.

A Solution to Hating Writing

If you'd rather be partying with friends or doing something other than writing, here are two suggestions. Hire a secretary and dictate your book, or employ a ghostwriter.

Chapter Eleven

Revisions and Critiques

Once you have finished have your first draft, you should take a 2 - 3 week break from writing that project.

If you start rewriting immediately, your mind tends to return to the images you had in your brain when you wrote the previous draft. It is important during rewrites that you READ the words on the page, not relive the creation process.

Reading your draft out loud is another method to force you into dealing only with on the words you have written. Also, hearing your sentences helps identify mistakes in grammar and punctuation.

I would suggest printing out the entire manuscript. There are inexpensive printing companies that can save you ink and paper cost.

I use a local shop that prints my files overnight for 3 cents a page. Printing a 300-page book costs only about $9. It might be worth the cost to get a copy made.

Reading a book from paper is different than using a computer. It also allows you to write notes in the margins.

Reviewing the Original Story Plan

There is no way, after creating over three hundred pages, that your original plot will remain intact. You either bend your draft back to that original idea or revise your story description into a new concept.

Typos, character-name mismatches and messed-up grammar will be sorted out as you review your work and listen to your critique group suggestions.

Are your scenes crisp, clear and well described, with a balance of dialogue, action, conflict and environment?

Review your story plan and revise it accordingly, then work on fixing the technical details while improving your dialogue and eliminating unnecessary words.

Microsoft's Review Tab

If you want to rewrite on computer, here is a suggestion. Take your finished file and save it as a new file like "Jaws notes for review". Then you can go to the review tab, in your Word 2010, almost to the center or the tool bar at the top. If you activate the "Track Changes" you can make temporary alterations to the manuscript and then "accept" or "reject" them later, and in addition, you can add a "New Comment." The comment is placed on the side of the text.

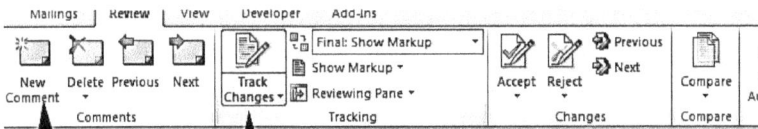

Making the Revision Plan

Working on a revision is not like creating a first draft. Entire scenes may be cut or rewritten, but many times the forward momentum is not as clear-cut as two pages a day. On average this is the progress you would want to make.

On the next page is a suggested time-table for a revision. The same place, same time, everyday routine needs to be continued.

Back to your Calendar

During the first week of your revision, make a general plan for the next six months. How many pages a week you are going to revise? How long are you going to work every day? Remember a goal without deadline is only a dream.

Help With the Revision

The revision process should definitely be done in conjunction with a critique group. New eyes and opinions need to be brought into the picture.

If you haven't already done so, this is the time to locate a critique group. You will need help during revisions to improve all aspects of your manuscript.

Care should be made in selecting a critique group. You want support, not criticism. You need readers to help you work with plot, sentence construction and clarity.

Week 1

Revisit your original fill-in-the-blank form and story description. Make sure your seven characters are still the primary ones in your story. Fix any diversions in the forms and rewrite the story description. Search for a suitable critique group.

Week 2

Read the entire book at about 15 - 20 pages a day. Do not get bogged down with rewriting. Make complete and legible notes. If something comes to mind for a later section do not go searching through the book for that location. Write that idea in a notebook with a description as to where it belongs and keep reading. Continue your search for a suitable critique group. Join one and test it out.

Week 3

Finish reading the entire book at about 15 - 20 pages a day. Make your final notes about the book's ending and plot. It is important to take the time to organize your notes in book order so you can make your changes efficiently. Revise your book description so you know exactly what you are now writing.

Weeks 4-26

Complete about two - five pages a day. At this point you will be doing two jobs; revising your book from the beginning, and working a different area of the book with your critique group. You will usually go faster through your rewrite than your critique group will read your material.

Weeks 11-22

Revise at about two - five pages a day, continue with critique group(s).

Weeks 22-26

Revise two - five pages a day, continue with critique group(s).

DATE	WEEK	JOB	✓	DATE	WEEK	JOB	✓
	1	Revisit the original story description and update it. Fix any changes in the forms. Find a critique group			15	Pages 141- 154	
	2	Read the entire book 15- 20 pages a day. Find a critique group.			16	Pages 155 - 168	
	3	Finish reading the book, make final notes about the ending and theme. Join a critique group. Review rules for submitting materials to the group.			17	Pages 169 - 182	
	4	Pages 1 - 14			18	Pages 183 - 196	
	5	Pages 15 - 28			19	Pages 197 - 210	
	6	Pages 29 - 42			20	Pages 211 - 224	
	7	Pages 43 - 56			21	Week of catch up	
	8	Pages 57 - 70			22	Pages 225 - 238	
	8	Pages 71 - 84			23	Pages 239 - 252	
	10	Pages 85 - 98			24	Pages 253- 266	
	11	Pages 99 - 112			25	Pages 267- 280	
	12	Week of catch up			26	Pages 281 - 294	
	13	Pages 113 - 126			27	Pages 295 - 308	
	14	Pages 127 - 140			28	Pages 295 - 308	

Adding Details

Rewriting is often a surgical process. It isn't about manically cutting and rewriting pages. Adding one sentence about a character's scar on her forearm, or the frost on the car's windshield can improve your story.

A wisp of hot apple pie on Christmas Eve or a distant, yet pungent cigar, the irritating scent of cheap perfume helps define characters and settings. Single sentences or an added phrase can bring new life to your story, cause readers to shed a tear or scare them.

Verbs Ending in "ing" Are Not Your Friend

The wording "Jackson was see**ing** the plane fall..." can be changed to "Jackson saw the plane fall..." Many verbs ending in "ing" are often "to be" words that can be elevated to powerful action verbs.

"She was runn**ing** past the tree..." can be improved to "She ran past the tree..." Consider more descriptive verbs rather than commonly used ones. "She stumbled, jogged, sprinted past the tree... "

The word "walk" can be replaced with "saunter, shuffle, stroll, limp, stride, sneak, or scamper." To paint a vivid picture use all the tools at your disposal.

Looking for a new word? In Windows computers, put your cursor on the word, right click and select Synonym. A list of alternatives will appear.

Doing a word search for "ing" can identify these verbs. Altering and improving "ing" words can make your manuscript much more interesting.

Watch out for "Nasty Words"

Here is a list of words that should be avoided in your book. Do a word search (F7 in windows MS Word 2010) and try to eliminate them. These words are overused and a waste of an opportunity for a more descriptive expression.

Very, almost, of course, involve, just, really, very, quite, sort of, walk, saw, seem, instantly, suddenly, briefly, good, bad, nice, went, came, moreover, a lot, all right, probably, words, is, are, was, were, be, been, being, make, made, involved, provide, provided that, look, heard, thought, 'ing' words, seemed as, got, get.

The Word Said is Invisible

The dialogue attribute said... "he said, she said." Is invisible to the reader. Although you will want to use descriptive dialogue attributes beside "said," it is not necessary to create unique attributes for every single line of dialogue.

Clichés, Technology, Time Stamps

Technology can lock a story into a time frame. Fax machines, disco balls, muskets, stagecoaches, steam engines, bulky computer CRTs, and bell bottoms often indicate specific years or social eras. Use technology and fashions with care and know what years they were employed.

Cell phones can be used in your novel, but we don't have to identify BlackBerrys, Razrs or iPhone4s. By the time your book is in print these devices may no longer exist. Having a character use outdated electronics can create an image of a backwards dork, which might not be what you intend.

Clichés and advertising slogans such as "Whazzzup!?!", "Where's the beef?" "Shazam!" "Right On!" and "Yeah, buddy!" can be used to lock in time, but these phrases can also go unrecognized by older or younger readers. It is best to write about people and their emotions. Those do not change.

Finding Your Critique Partner(s)

You cannot rewrite alone. It is virtually impossible to identify all the typos, wrong word choices, plot holes and mismatched issues in a book. You will need help.

This help can come from many directions: trusted readers, critique groups, fellow writers, or (maybe) family members, but be particular about who you choose.

Your readers must understand the type of book you are writing and that you are looking for help, not criticism. All too often a beginning writer is crushed under the "supportive" advice like this:

"You really should write a story about Aunt May. All this murder and detective talk is boring."

Or:

"I don't like your main character's name, and you should make her a vampire. That's what really sells. "

It's your book, your idea, your time. Treat it like gold.

Who is writing this Book?

An amazing thing happens during the writing process: creativity takes over from your conscious mind. You might begin writing one story and another emerges.

The only way to get to the heart of your book is to finish it. If at any time you feel blocked, return to your character descriptions or scene forms and there will be a conflict that you have not fully explored.

If your story changes, fix it on the rewrite. When do you start over? When the book you began no longer exists: the plot has changed, the main character has changed , the locations and time period have changed. You will have to open a new file and start the entire process over. This is an entirely new book.

You'll probably need a new workbook, too.

The Rewrite – Path to Greatness

A first draft is usually riddled with errors and mistakes. Do not worry. A great book is built, not born. It is like a statue that is roughed out, cut into a defined shape and then sanded in just the right places.

The original script for the movie "Star Wars" went through many versions. Look it up on Wikipedia. Do not think your first idea is your best...or your last.

The rewrite is where bravery comes into play. It takes courage to cut superfluous and redundant dialogue as the page count shrinks. It takes stepping back and visualizing that scene. What's that on the floor? Whose eye twitches, and is that a crow sitting on her gravestone or is it a vulture?

Smells – decaying leaves and fresh dirt mixed with...what is that familiar scent?

A torn cuff, an unexplained scratch on her thigh, and an unusually cold breeze from the south all add to the mood, your character's image and the reader's experience.

We often fall in love with our words, but many times we do not write what we see in our mind's eye. Carefully tucking descriptions between paragraphs, thoughts between dialogue, small actions among the large, and rewrites are the path to greatness.

Spell Check doesn't check usage

Spell check in a word processor cannot always figure the right use between "your" and "you're," between "it's" and "its" and between "who's" and "whose." Quotes can be mismatched. There is a difference between an en dash (-) and an em dash (–) and where they are used.

It important that someone who copyedits for a living read and correct your manuscript before you start handing it out. An author can never catch all the errors in his own writing.

Preparing for Agents and Publishers

The 3by3 Writing Method believes the most profitable path to writing success is forming an alliance with professionals in the publishing business. Only after an exhaustive search for representation and/or a publisher should an author head into the self-publishing world.

It is no longer expensive or difficult to become a published author. <u>Selling</u> a book is the greatest challenge that an author faces, aside from properly finishing it.

Every title, fiction and non-fiction, is a competitor for a book buyer's dollar. This is why having a publisher's acceptance is the first choice of the 3by3 Writing Method.

However, if a publisher offers a contract, the author must remain actively involved. A successful author will work with their publisher in terms of social media, marketing and pursuing media interest.

A publisher and an author can use publicity, marketing, the Internet and bookstore presence to take full advantage of all the possibilities available for selling a title. Nothing beats having a publishing company promoting, marketing and distributing your work.

Self-publishing a book is a task that requires additional time, money and energy. You might hear and read inspiring stories of a self-published author making a big splash and even bigger sales; being wildly successful and working at home. They are the few lucky self-publishing stories. .

The second workbook in the 3by3 Writing Method Series details the search for an agent and publisher as well as and preparing the manuscript for publication

.

Chapter Twelve

Author Resources

Here are some valuable resources you might want to explore..

Funds for Writers

Funds for Writers is a great website that offers tips on writing, scholarships, publisher information, and agents seeking clients. Signing up will put you on their email list, and you will get informative messages quite often.

http://www.fundsforwriters.com/

Preditors and editors

This website is a must for any writer who's serious about landing an agent or publisher. Not only does it list agents and scam/agents, it has a host of other information.

http://pred-ed.com/

Writer's Market

When it is time to search for agents or publishers, this online resource is invaluable. Of course you will have to double-check every agent or publisher by visiting their website and examining their status at Preditors and Editors, but it is a perfect website for that beginning search. It costs a little money, but it is worth it.

Writersmarket.com

Meetup.com

I run a Meetup.com critique group. There are other meetup.com groups focused on writing that meet all over the country. Some groups are aimed at screenwriters or poets. Others are not so specific. Some are designed for critiques, some are social gatherings. You might look into this website as a way to connect with writers in your area.

Meetup.com

Critters.org

Critters.org is an online critique site for writers. I hesitate to suggest that anyone submit a full book or project online, but this is a place to start with portions of your current draft. Because you do not know the experience or motivation of online readers, be wary. Always protect your work.

Criters.org

Write good or die

As of this writing, the book "Write Good or Die" is available on Amazon.com and is free to download to a Kindle program or device. It is a compilation of essays on writing. Very good reading.

Amazon.com

Open Office

Open office is a free office productivity suite that includes a powerful word processor. It is not MS Word, and has its own quirks, but for getting a job done, the price (free) is right.

Openoffice.org

Website for conferences

http://www.newpages.com/writing-conferences/ is a website that lists writer's conferences. It is a great idea to network with other writers, agents and editors.

newpages.com/writing-conferences/

3by3 Writing Method Resources

If you want more information or just want to keep up-to-date with the 3by3 Writing Method, here are some places to visit. -

Blog & website - 3by3writingmethod.com.

Blog - 3by3writingmethod.wordpress.com

Follow us on twitter - @3by3writer.

Facebook - Threebythree Writingmethod

Last Words

Having your book published is one of the most exhilarating feelings in the world. It does not happen often, so when it does, revel in the moment.

Good luck, and keep writing!

THE 3BY3 WRITING METHOD - BOOK ONE
PLAN, WRITE AND FINISH YOUR NOVEL

1. Write Daily at a Dedicated Time and Place

    1.1 Write at the same time every day.

    1.2 Write in the same place every day.

    1.3 Work for the same length of time every day.

2. Constant Contained Conflict (CCC)

    2.1 Characters are conflicted internally.

    2.2 Characters have conflicts with each other.

    2.3 Characters have ties to each other; financially, through family or some binding tie that confines and constrains them.

3. Finish a typo-free, properly formatted manuscript

    3.1 The manuscript is properly formatted and has gone through at least two comprehensive drafts.

    3.2 The manuscript has been read by at least one reader and/or a critique group familiar with your genre.

    3.3 At least one professional pass has been made to correct spelling, formatting and grammar.

About the Author

Steven E. Browne self-published one of the first books on computerized video editing. "The Post-Production Primer" was quickly adopted by several well-known universities.

Browne revised "The Post-Production Primer" for the technical publisher Focal Press. "Video Editing" continued its original success being the primary text for many more university and commercial post-production classes. Browne wrote several additional books for Focal Press. "Video Editing" went through four full editions in its fifteen years of publication.

Browne's sci-fi novel, "Protecting the Source" received an enthusiastic review from the American Library Journal. The book sold out its initial print run and was pitched to several movie studios.

His second novel, "Holly Would, But Stacy Won't," is a quirky love story about a cynical novelist being ensnared by a couple of female movie producers with murder on their minds.

Steven E. Browne is no stranger to publishing. He has self-published using offset printing, perfect bound, spiral bound, print-on-demand, and eBook. He lives in the Pasadena, California area and writes every day.

www.ingramcontent.com/pod-product-compliance
Lightning Source LLC
Chambersburg PA
CBHW051811040426
42446CB00007B/622